The Beginning of the One

By

King Saul Real Negus

Copyright © King Saul Real Negus

All rights reserved. No part of this publication may be reproduced, distributed, or transmitted in any form or by any means, including photocopying, recording, or other electronic or mechanical methods, without the prior written permission of the publisher, except in the case of brief quotations embodied in critical reviews and certain other noncommercial uses permitted by copyright law.

ISBN-13: 978-1-951300-29-6

Liberation's Publishing ~ West Point, Mississippi

Greetings with Peace, Love, and Light.

I wholeheartedly acknowledge our ancestors and my guardian angel for this message to awaken our people with this conscious information. Also, thanks to my doubters and motivators. Thanks to my family who really did time with me and helped. Thanks for the discipline, dedication, and determination. To Growth & Development and Positive, Productive Minds.

Contents

Introduction 11

Mind Mechanic 13

The Beginning of the One 17

All I Want Is What's Mine 21

Change 22

Growth 23

Knowledge 24

How Do You Teach Without the Interference of Slave Teaching? 26

Creativity 29

Brainwashing 31

Own Your Mind Process Reality 33

Reality Prison 35

Reincarnated 36

One Love, One Heart, One Mind 37

Courage and Confidence 39

Teaching Self 41

- The Center of Creation ... 43
- Programming ... 45
- Growing Up in The Matrix ... 46
- Self-Motivation ... 47
- Unity ... 47
- No Handout ... 49
- Fear ... 50
- Speaking Life ... 51
- Mislead ... 51
- Melanin ... 52
- Mental Chains ... 53
- Breaking Generational Curses ... 54
- The Strength of Thinking on One Accord ... 55
- Thoughts ... 56
- The Power of Thy Name ... 57
- Letters to King Hoover ... 58
- Letters to My Brothers ... 60
- Letter to Chubby ... 61

To My Big Brother 61

Princess Chloe 63

Letter to Mother Queen's Day 65

Queen's Day 2 67

Love Letter to Self 68

Blessed 69

Spiritual Guidance 69

Materialistic Things Don't Impress Me, Your Soul Does 69

One Generation 70

Spiritual 71

I Know My Language 71

Unnatural Teaching 72

Two Roads of Life 72

Peace 73

My Wealth 73

Manifesting 74

Existence 74

Conscious of Life 75

Heaven State of Mind 76

Respect 77

Eye Am My Ancestors 78

Belief System 79

I Am 80

Queen Dione 81

Letter to my Queen 81

Never Surrender 82

Three Things You Can't Hide for Long 83

You Create 84

Healing 84

Queens and Kings 85

Love Africa 86

Mindset 87

MAC 88

Wake Up 89

Transformation 90

Discrimination	91
God's Hands	92
Grand Risings	92
Ancestor's Prayer	93

Introduction

My name is Charles Wayne Saul Jr., born from "One of the Greatest Minds" on March 8, 1992, 10:10 am. I'm writing my story as a God of the 1b8m Gods and Goddesses today. My life will be the perfect example of who we are. My position is the Sun of the family. I Am a Seer. The Light, this Light shall be forever Lit in Our Hearts and Minds. I come to you as my personality changes and grows still. I wasn't always aware of this information or woke or aware of life. But curious, I couldn't stop wondering, something wasn't adding up. My life started off rough from false teachings, and I'm not here to blame anyone for my being misled. I have no idea where or when the deception started.

My Point is, I Love My Family and I Am here to break all generational curses. I love helping family and others. My energy and strength it must be balanced. Honestly, this feels great, learning myself. How did this happen? Well, August 22, 2020, I didn't get released from prison and went rogue. I was outraged for about a month, not believing anything I was told. The facts didn't add up. Oh well—basically I was giving up. I threw my bibles away and walked away from all religious beliefs. What I did do was start seeing truth. I did research on any and everything and still do to this day. I have always been intelligent since I was young and noticed I always had this talent of creativity.

See, now I know more of my spiritual self and see me as my vessel/temple. I taught myself meditation and started reading and researching. I had to understand to believe, simply, you always know right if you're indeed righteous. Creating is like a drug to my mind because of its continuous expansion to grow. We are all natural creators.

This is spiritual work now, working for self, the one mind which we all originated from. Family, keep the Peace.

I Am

King Saul

Real Negus

Mind Mechanic

04/12/2021

You may wonder how I found my spirituality and Black intelligence in prison with the help of our ancestors and my guardian angel. To start, I grew up in West Point, Mississippi, The Golden Triangle Area, where my life started off rough, without a culture and no knowledge of self. I was dazed at what I was told about life while growing up. I was never submissive to adapt to the environment, I only went down the wrong road, doing illegal things, which led me to prison. My Angels had to save a man's life not once but twice. First, it was like I was in a dream. I was pulling the trigger with direct aim, but the gun didn't shoot. Unconscious me didn't realize the message and went to get another gun. I wanted this man's life for his disrespectful actions. Thankfully, nobody got hurt and I only had to sit down almost seven years for my actions. That's the reason why I'm incarcerated now, soon to be released. I forgave him and those others who played on my morality. That was how I got to prison. I was merely on the wrong path to destruction. I was projecting in darkness, cause and effect.

Days before the above incident that led me to

prison, I agreed to take someone else's contraband in broad daylight. I got away, but do you see the cause and effect, Family? Asé.[1] I always loved to create and produce music and was always trying to further my music career. While in prison, I met back up with the person I stole the contraband from. We squashed that foolishness, and we will soon be able to aid each other in our music careers.

Born into a family of four brothers, I was what you may have called the problem child without a big support system. Honestly, I was always looking for understanding but was taught falsely. For me school was like daycare. I even remember being asked to explain to the class how I had solved a mathematical equation. My thought was, "shouldn't the teacher have been doing that?" I was always searching for the truth, as in knowledge of our history and culture. You will only accept false teachings if you refuse to know yourself. Truth is already in our DNA. We just have to raise our level of conscious and find ourselves. I came about great knowledge from the motherland, researching and finding books explaining things I do and am interested in. I'm not racist. I just don't have

---

[1] Ase is a West African philosophical concept through which the Yoruba of Nigeria conceive the power to make things happen and produce change. We all mean we're in agreement.

sympathy to those who force unnatural ways on our people. Nor, to those who hold our intellectual properties, knowledge, and our culture histories hostage. My message is merely for our people. We've all been lied to and need enlightenment to wake up. Are we going to continually accept and settle for nothing? Well, I been made my mind up to grow and develop and searching of truth. Peace.

The Beginning of the One

12/09/2020

    Today was a great day. It made my third day not smoking marijuana for no particular reason. One[2] noticed this wasn't even a challenge to stop. It was basic mind control. One has control over this vessel. One understands this now, and One is a 28-year-old vessel who awakened to see this world as it is. One also is learning a lot at a rapid speed. Notice that it's one because I am becoming one with the universe. Knowledge is the true power.

    Peace be family. 2021 is the year of my release back into society. This is my year of one success into my spiritual connections. Success with my family. One now notices the creators and the creator in oneself. One is now discovering the power of meditation and manifestation. One is the creator. One has the power to create his life story. Creativity with positivity is righteousness.

Goals for 2021

- Self-education - learn the history of our ancestors and the science and math of right

---

[2] The beginning of me becoming one with the Universe.

knowledge.

- Being a great sponsor, a caring, providing, and protecting father for my princess, Chloe.

- Building my first studio and independently start a lucrative record label in the music business.

- Starting an education system of right knowledge for the Black communities.

- Practicing unity amongst the Black communities and civilization.

- Helping awaken as many as possible to gain full control of our minds.

Manifestations 12/23/2020

- I Am asserting the master of the real self.
- I Am using my willpower.
- I Am mastering the law of attraction.
- I Am disciplining this vessel (flesh).
- I have discovered the I Am.

More Goals for 2021

- Be united in Peace.
- Progress in spiritual growth.
- Progress in my vessel's aspirations.
- First unity and peace with the Family.
- Production of Ancient Love.
- Procreation of Legacy of Righteousness Positives, clothing companies, Record label, Right Knowledge, Real Estate, Schools, Black civilization, Fatherhood, Connections, Overstanding Health, Success, Currency Aspirations, Master Thoughts, Entrepreneur.
- From this date on, its growth, fruitful in the physical, financial, and spiritual worlds

The Lying Tongue 12/26/2020

- There are ways around a lying tongue.
- You can't beat lies with words, only actions.
- Kindness is a deadly weapon against your enemy. You don't play the foolish game of argument; it only insults your intelligence.
- Mind tactics are the true muscles.

All I Want Is What's Mine

Stop Being the Joke

And Look More into You

Search for The Truth

A lot of Things Ain't you

Do You Celebrate Holidays

'Cause It's The Truth,

or 'Cause you were Told to?

Give Us Back Our Minds

and We'll Stay Divine

All I Want Is What's Mine!!!

Change

12/30/2020

It is about time for change. The year of change is 2021, so instead of fearing change, embrace it. Change, a majority of the time, is for the better. Change your environment from negative into positive. Your thought patterns attract like-minded individuals, so if you're thinking negative all the time you will attract negative things and attract negative company, and vice versa. Turn away from toxic relationships and energy vampires. The toxic person thrives to drain you because of their miserable state. They always blame others, never taking responsibility.

Practice creating better positive thoughts in the thought world. Positive thoughts create a positive world. Remember, thoughts are actions.

Growth

01/06/2021

I should not put anything before the creator and me. This Vessel is as a plant, and I am to grow fruitful and multiply. Knowledge is food for the soul. Yeah, that's right, knowledge. We are spiritually poor and must recover and renew our minds to change our way of thinking. Say this with me and mean it: I Am Alive. And repeat this hourly, positively, and also during activities such as before eating exercises, etc. Hold on to that thought. I want us Kings and Queens to be awakened to our right state. Also, hold on to these words as such energy and indivisible determination.

My Kings and Queens, we have to let go of fear and its family. Why would you feed negative thoughts or worry about trouble to come in the future? You master your thoughts positively and take control of your destiny. Wait on no one, but simply take control. There is no one coming to save you. Reprogram your mind, let it all go, and let your heart lead the way. We are our saviors, and I am the light.

Knowledge

01/13/2021

Knowledge is in our DNA. We only have to unlock such parts of the mind for right knowledge and get in tune with our inner self's voice. For guidance and help, contact the Sun, The Highest Source of Energy, or eat Sun grown food, which sends out info through thought waves at 432 or higher frequencies. Yeah, thoughts connect to this frequency of the like-minded. Become one with the Universe. Your thoughts will manifest and become reality with ease unexpectedly. But remember, if you're feeding fear and worry, you are living backwards. EVIL, FLIP IT TO LIVE. OR "DEVIL" STATE AKA Negative State, once turned around, you "LIVED" STATE AKA Positive state of mind, which we want.

Stop being the joke and look more into what the majority are following and start asking some questions. Search for the truth. There are a lot of things you can ask your own parents. For example, why do we celebrate Christmas? Their response is going to be their parents celebrated it when they were kids. We are all following something of which no one ever understood or was aware of what it actually was at the time. Family, we gotta stop that way of thinking. Unknowingly, someone else programmed our subconscious thoughts. Like autosuggestions in the mind, the blind leading the blind.

How Do You Teach Without the Interference of Slave Teaching?

First you must separate from their unnatural way of thinking, living, lusting, fear, etc. Their concept is in order for their riches someone must be poor. My concept is in order for our riches we must grow in unity as a family. Give them back their slave books, education, culture, etc. The lack of love for self and your own life. You start looking for attention and sometimes maybe invading on someone else's life. The ignorant think they make themselves better by tricknology, accusing others, playing victim, separating themselves from the Black Nation.

We as a whole are of pure light, love, peace, righteousness, health, wonderful things by Divine right. Wickedness, deception, hatred, enviousness must be destroyed out the mind along with destruction and greed.

Our queens want to downgrade themselves to a lower status subconsciously, following the media's wicked agenda and everything that glitters. They want to merely be eye candy, which is poisonous to the soul. Our queens used to rule and conquer empires. They still generate offspring, which is questionable to me of how it really all started. Also questionable, can our queens produce life independently in their original state?

Our kings also want to be like someone else instead of themselves, subconsciously killing off our race and dehumanizing our vessels. Especially our Black women, who want to be everything but themselves with those wigs, fake eyelashes, butt shots, etc. Mental slavery is in plain sight and also, why and where? Why we don't have a culture of our own, so-called African Americans. Where and what happened to our Real History? Why did they rearrange the seasons away from the original moon cycle, and why do they celebrate New Year's in the midst of winter when it's really not until March? January and February are add-on months. It used to be ten days a week and ten months a year.

They don't want you in tune with yourselves and the Universe for some reason. Are they afraid of something? That's why they tell you to pray to someone, something outside of yourself in this Game of Life, overlooking the Gods and Goddesses in plain sight.

- Who is they? All parties involved in the unnatural acts.

- Realize I am God/Goddess. I admit that I am powerful to control my tendency to do the right thing and that my life is manageable.

Creativity

1/20/2021

Be creative, Kings and Queens. Be the change. Change your thought patterns and start searching for the truth, ask questions. Manifest your own reality. Unsubscribe to whatever and everything you've been attached to because you were told to and make your own channel. We the willing we can do very much with little, simply by using our willpower and attracting those things which we all inherited.

Grow into your own person of interest and stop trying to be or be like someone else.

Brainwashing

02/10/2021

The fear-based reality created by the opposition of nature also created a wicked language of curses. Which is to be decoded and reinterpreted. They also control the media, which isolates us from former associates and sources of information. What some fail to realize is they are using us to manifest their wickedness. Telling us their falsehoods and ideology for centuries till the point of deception of a whole nation. Then it's legal to brainwash people, only not against the ethical laws. If it was illegal, then TV, movies, books, articles, speeches, advertising, lectures, school, sermons, and communication in general would be banned. Right, it's fair game.

Their doctrine and belief system are wicked and plain wrong. They done LIED to our parents' parents to further their agenda. It now has come to a stopping point to stop those liars and deceivers. Time to step outside our comfort zone and search the truth and ask, why? Rebel against their agenda; it's only leading us into destruction.

Own Your Mind Process Reality

03/22/2021

Family, we have to consciously reprogram our subconscious mind. Our subconscious mind is that 90% they tell us nothing about. Example: Things you do without thinking, like blinking your eyes. We have picked up on unnatural ways that we need curing to our minds. Remember, we are powerful Gods and Goddesses in this game. So, by installing positive, productive habits, you are training your sub-thoughts for the better. You don't want to be carrying on wickedness to the next generations. By doing so, our youth will be more powerful and productive in this way.

Reality Prison

03/02/2021 and 03/03/2021

Some people and some parents unknowingly imprisoned themselves to financial slavery. They tried to force this type of slavery on the young, telling them they need a job to live, and dedicated their whole life following someone else's dream thought of business. But they realized how much time they didn't have for themselves and their dreams. They were always complaining about their own jobs. We should not live like this. We should love our work as our worship and be joyful doing so. I'm not going to force my kids to this slavery. Twelve hours on the job, eight hours of sleep, one hour driving, one hour cooking, and maybe even two hours for yourself. Ladies and gentlemen, this isn't our way of living, Gods/Goddesses.

Those creative ideas and dreams of your kids should be pursued and not overlooked, or you shouldn't be telling a God/Goddess they can't do some things. You should be more creative and create your own source of work that you love. We are natural creators who have this creative energy (black germ ether). We only need to learn ourselves and how to use this energy.

Reincarnated

03/08/1992

    Twenty-nine years ago, my personality was created as you know of today. Thankfully, I'm alive and consciously aware of life. On my journey within learning thyself, I discovered I'm a seer. One of the lights to enlighten those who are asleep to the truth. It's my duty of purpose.

    I

    Am

    King

One Love, One Heart, One Mind

03/10/2021

From the beginning, there was one mind, the God Mind, which expanded from 1 to 2 to 3 to 7 to 12. The 12 Tribe Elders expanded to 144, then to 144000, and finally to the 1 billion 8 million Gods and Goddesses we are today. Family, we gotta stop looking for something outside of us and go within thyself. Family, we were once all connected, still in the One God Mind. Gods and Goddesses, know your relationship with your family and start back looking and accepting the truth as it is. Gods and Goddesses are all brothers and sisters who need to be reunited and unified again. Peace.

Courage and Confidence

03/17/2021

Your confidence shows the strength in your character, it defines who you are. Be confident in your dreams, goals, and purposes. Remember, your character is you, so nobody dictates you or your reality, no matter how many doubters and envious individuals are around. Apparently, they just want your spot. We have the courage (you are reading this book), have the courage to walk it like you talk it defining your character 100% when practice means living word from word in action.

When practice in righteousness see the results, so will those lie you're trying to live up to hindering your growth. Family, know the difference between aging and growing, because you can be an 80-year-old vessel with a sixth month-old mentality. Like, since six months of age, you were taught lies, meaningless lies, which hinder the growth of your character, your true self. Then, 80 years pass by, and you figured out you were lied to the whole time. So, you only aged 80 years without growth. Peace.

Teaching Self

It's possible to teach yourself if you've been lied to. You have got to pay that inner voice some attention. Me personally, a lot of things never set right with me since early school, which was practically forced on us. So, I was always searching for truth and endured my share of trials and tribulations being rebellious to the system. Sometimes, your own parents act as agents for the system unknowingly. I've always known those school teachings were false for the Gods. Up to ninth grade, the school year was just daycare for me, only learning the percentage of truth allowed.

I am writing this book from prison. I went through phases of analysis and comparing information until my inner self heart the righteousness, the truth. I always look at the big media as a show, just like the circus, never seriously. Meaning the news and TV shows were clown shows and staged acts. I couldn't look up to my oppressors and nevertheless, settled for nothing. If my heart can't accept something, neither can I.

The Center of Creation

The pure black germ ether is the substance that creates from nothing. This is what makes us so unique and creative. The ability to create out of thin space. The ether is what you see at night, that magical blackness, and what's seen once your eyes are closed. How powerful are we to do such things to create universes, solar systems, star systems, planets, etc.? How powerful is our God Mind in unity once unified again? How did we come from creating universes, etc., to slaves on our own earth? Somehow, we've all been hit with a cute case of amnesia, but it's time to wake up and get yours back.

Black is the center of Creation. It represents all colors of existence, vibrance, etc. Without Black, there wouldn't be any white, 'because white comes from removing the black germ completely, creating a sub-human (children) race. Black is the beginning with no end. So, explain to me how your children became your masters? From my perspective, once the God Mind expanded and became individual Gods and Goddesses, we downgraded our morals someway, being forgetful, and created the sub-human race that turned against us. In actuality, all things have opposite sides, as you can see. Our opposite is unnatural beings, like the people or races that are dying from the natural Sun. These are scientific facts.

From my perspective, they couldn't get energy from the direct source and created artificial intelligence, religious, fear, etc., to drain the original Gods of their energy. That's why in their teachings, they want you to be fearful and blind in ignorance (sleep). Teaching you to fear yourself, which a number of us are still doing today, fearing God. Notice the events created in 2020 by the unnatural to empower their wicked agenda, and a lot of people are fearing right into their game plan of dehumanization. Yes, the v shot is the whole key of the virus. Like running an entire flock off a cliff into destruction. Trick the people with fear into signing their death certificate with that nanotechnology, which empowers their network of AI.

Programming

The best time to start training the mind is when one is a child, when the conscious mind is very pliable, but one can do it as an adult also. The key to success is to be aware that super learning or recalling is like making a path through a field by constantly walking it. Once this idea becomes clear in mind, then the training plan will succeed. Keep pencil and paper next to your bed and write down your dreams every morning in as much detail as possible and keep a daily journal.

With no writing, children are trained and asked by adults to recall dreams and their days' adventures when sitting around the home fire at night. Children are never discouraged from indulging in their imaginary worlds. Once they grow older and eventually become adults, they retain this power of vivid imagination and bring it under complete mental control.

We Black people made the other races in our image, and 6000 years ago is when all the troubles on earth started. We must be taught separately. Why do people get mad at you for speaking the truth rather than being mad at who lied to us? Don't even be mad, have no sympathy for the unnaturals. Do your business and carry on and continue to be peaceful.

Growing Up in The Matrix

Growing up in the Matrix as a kid is very difficult. For me, I was placed in a school where I felt unwanted and out of place. The Matrix doesn't teach, it only tells, and will use anyone to try and keep you programmed. So, they'll tell your parents things they feel are good for you, and once your parents agree, it's doomed. I'm sad to say, but everyone is not awaking, and while they are asleep, they are in a robotic mindset. Parents don't even listen or interact with their children and feel they are grownups, so you have no voice or say so whatsoever. I know you remember hearing a lot, "these are grownups talking, go play."

This is plainly foolishness and forgetfulness, which we need to do away with. In actuality, kids are born fearless. It is the adults and their slave masters who instill fear. Thankfully, I never gave in to letting them tell me what they wanted me to be and what I can be. Surely, I was punished for my rebellious acts, but nevertheless, I was unbroken. The confidence I held as a minor is empowering me now, and my dream was always there.

Self-Motivation

Once you realize your true self, you are meeting your number one motivator. That inner voice that is always saying something told me to do something. Start listening and paying attention.

Nobody is going to do it better than your God Self. Once you realize this, you'll be successful in life.

Unity

There is power in unity. Two or more minds are always more powerful. Once you have a unified circle, you become untouchable and accomplished more quickly. We all are reincarnated Gods/Goddesses, expansion of the One God Mind. How powerful is the mind?

No Handout

Listen carefully. Now, we all are creators, if you educate yourself on yourself. There is no way to be a dependent to the system. This book being read was created from the creative black gene (germ). Knowledge from the mind to this paper/screen is an example of creations from nothing. Another example of using this gene is when you're having sex connected in one mind and create life. Being dependent is a form of laziness picked up unnaturally. Start working for your God Self like I am now. Peace.

Fear

Fear can interrupt processes in our brains that allow us to regulate emotions, memories, and self-control. Read to educate self and be aware of other information presented to us; think before you react. Fear impacts our thinking and decision making in negative ways, leaving us susceptible to intense emotions and impulsive reactions. Once you overcome fear, you can see clearly.

Parents, you know the ones I'm speaking about, stop doing your slave master's job, instilling fear to the youth, stripping them of their innocent and vivid imagination. Notice they also strip animals of their innocent livelihood wrongfully because of their evil greed of business and money. So, be more considerably aware of what's at hand. Be the change. Peace.

Speaking Life

So, how many of you ever heard of speaking life into existence? Some of you may have experienced things of which you've spoken. This is indeed true, but now is the time to speak life consciously being aware. Walking the talk is very powerful. Once you gain back control of your mind and accept the fact that we've been lied to, Life becomes easier in truth. The truth shall set you free. Peace.

Mislead

Notice how the system taught you to follow and not to lead. Question which classes teach about self. Why we weren't taught about numerology and astronomy. Family, Gods/Goddesses, we have been taught not to trust ourselves and taught self-hatred. They teach us to wanna be instead of being. Self-awareness is a superpower.

Melanin

I love this Black power

my Black color

Who are those to tell me other?

See my heart is pure

Melaninated Never penetrated

So those who hated,

Congratulations

You also helped pave the way

See, Melanin is better than any Material things

With a heart that sings

Can't nothing come in between

Divine Unity Please

Keep The Peace

Mental Chains

Spirituality vs religion. It's a major difference. Our spirit deserves the best and is to roam and grow freely in our world, not contained or trapped to such false teachings. Like keeping your mind trapped inside a box when we can roam the universe freely. Once I left the religious box and started my journey in spirituality, I was reminded of my gifts and skills by my ancestors. Also, once they helped me find the queen in Africa, I immediately realize how powerful we are. Peace.

Self-Hate Will End When Knowledge of Self Begins

See, the strong mind always wins when travelling within, so keep striving, Ladies and Gentlemen. Gods-Goddesses, one is best, one is all we need. Peace.

Breaking Generational Curses

If a man and woman don't save money together, they're not passing their lineage, kingdom, or empire down to their children. If God made Eve for Adam, Eve is supposed to be Adam's rib, right? So, they're supposed to be one flesh, one body. I will never understand why the Adams and Eves in this modern day and era won't use those same aspects towards the materialistic things of this world. You want love, but don't want to be on one accord with your partner. To be a King or Queen, you must do things in order. In marriage, Kings and Queens always did things together. Mostly likely, if you're not moving like a King or Queen, your family structure or household is going through a generational curse.

The Strength of Thinking on One Accord

This strength applied with multiple individuals thinking in unity is how to build pyramids. The unified mind can do anything righteously. More minds mean bigger achievements in unity. So, come up with a plan, write it out, then gather your other minds and all picture the plan on one accord, all feeding the thought, and apply actions.

Thoughts

When thoughts are big, they take time to grow as a big, beautiful tree would. Your mind and person are to water your thoughts by focusing on feeding those thoughts. Meditation could help, but simply, the same imagination you had when you were younger was real, but just developing life, living experiences, growing. Once matured is the developing stage, so how much gas do you put in your car? How much do you feed that thought? 'Cause it's time for abundance and prosperity now.

The Power of Thy Name

The power we hold is immeasurable and actually works easy for us. Like Facebook likes, get you some believers of yourself and y'all think on a unified level. The power is amazing. Your words are powerful, rightfully used, and applied with rightful actions. I do have believers myself. Peace.

Living

Live your life freely and learn through experiences and guidance from the angelic realms. Only we can teach each other righteousness of life.

Letters to King Hoover

Thanks for the unity and peace

The Discipline, dedication

The loyalty and love

The honor and respect To All Gods on Deck

With Smiles to Perfect

We Shine We Shine No More Stressing

No More Tears

No More Lies No More Fears Free Hoover

We Know

Who We Is

Letters to My Brothers

Bro, I seen us sitting around

You had NHG Representatives present

I Gave Y'all The Game

You going to sign all as yours

As a Family in Unity, Divine Unity We Win in Family, In One Mind Only Positive Minds

Strong Minds

Letter to Chubby

Only the strong survive

To Family, We Live in Divine Strength in One Mind, We Shine

Natural Warriors in Glory Peacefully Still

'Cause Harm Will Kill See my Family I Love From under to above

No More Worries, No More Fears Just Believe and We Will Live

To My Big Brother

Bro, We Did It

Minds are made to expand With a Mind to Build

We Live, We Live with Love with Mind in One Mind

Princess Chloe

My love, you are the best

You are strong, you are beautiful Even when wrong

It's Been so Long, we strong

I'm Coming Home with You Where I Belong

My Love for You Has Grown Entirely Renewed and Strong My Protection to Chloe's

I'll Never Lead You Wrong.

Letter to Mother Queen's Day

Blessings to The Mother

Who Is Queen?

Blessed Is the Hearts

That Follow Dreams

Thanks For the Creations

Of These Kings

Thanks For Your love

Of Y'all Making Me

Happy Queen Day

Peace Love Light

Queen's Day 2

Blessings To the Queen

Who Bear Seeds of Me

Blessed Is That Seed

Who Sprung Complete

Thanks For the Love

With Plenty More to Give

Blessings Upon Us

Two Hearts to Heal

Happy Queen Day

Peace Love Light

Love Letter to Self

Letter From Me

I Set You Free

Growth To Seek

My Dreams to Meet

Thanks For the Love

Thanks For the Gifts

Thanks To Divinity

No More Hardships

Blessed

I have wonderful businesses in a wonderful way. I give wonderful services for wonderful pay.

Spiritual Guidance

I am always under direct inspiration. I make right decisions quickly. I will let the will of God be done.

Materialistic Things Don't Impress Me, Your Soul Does

I'm not the type to be bought. Once you know your ownership of this world, it'll be easy if you understand everything is already yours. You forgot we all created this with Black power. We shall not want what's already ours.

One Generation

Ours is to reveal the truth and reverse the brainwashing. I had a vision of purchasing a school for our culture and youth. To educate and wake does help you understand who you are. If your path is more difficult, it's because your calling is higher. Your ancestors are waiting on you to connect. Power to our people. We are strong, living examples.

Spiritual

When a spirit gives you a gift, even if it's just a voice, take it with gratitude. It may be the only thing they got to give, and they choose to give it to you. When the spirit is happy, the mind and body will follow.

I Know My Language

Family, our communications are mental. By connecting globally, we change global things. We are powerful to think with the universe, becoming one with the universal mind. Our words, actions, and specifically our writings, are powerful. Please identify yourself to this world wholeheartedly.

Unnatural Teaching

They call spirituality of our ancestor's madness. We are spiritual people, but many of you have forgotten and became religious from the unnatural false doctrines.

Two Roads of Life

There are two roads on which a human being could go, one of wisdom and one of ignorance. The path of the masses is generally the path of ignorance, which leads to negative situations, thoughts, and deeds. These in turn lead to ill health and sorrow in life. The other road is based on wisdom, and it leads to health, true happiness, and enlightenment. I practice our culture cause our ancestors weren't allowed to. If one doesn't have awareness of the lower self, one can't evolve into one's higher self.

Peace

It does not mean to be in a place where there is no noise, trouble, or hard work. It means to be in the midst of those things and still be calm in heart. Fearless.

My Wealth

My wealth is the knowledge of self, love, and spirituality. It feels great to be entitled to the riches of life. To think in the same mind as the universe.

We are not separate from the whole, we are one with the sun, earth, and the air. We don't have a life, we are Life. This is our world.

Manifesting

- When manifesting, keep a positive mindset.
- Live it.
- See it.
- Breathe it.
- If it's real in mind, it's indeed real.

Existence

Everything that exists is spirit. It's either spirit or doesn't exist. Material things are merely manifestations of spirit. Spirit is the fundamental reality.

Conscious of Life

A conscious person always self-reflects, questions themselves, recognizes their mistakes, and tries to correct them. Being conscious with life feels great. The idea is to raise your level of consciousness. Instead of being forgetful, you train to be in a state of remembrance. Search to understand life. I found knowledge in meditation. I freed myself also and learned these things I teach now. I have reached the heavens mentally and I'm hands on to the highest power, no middlemen are needed. I'm plugged in with the world. We should identify ourselves wholeheartedly.

Everybody has that one ancestor who ain't for nobody's games.

Heaven State of Mind

This heavenly state of mind I have is the best. This is just a manuscript of my vessel. We are highly intelligent and only we can teach us. My Angels guide me in all righteous ways and brought me miracles and power. I am here today to show the way and to light the flames in our hearts and minds.

Respect

When your ancestors come to dance with you, get up and dance. Our ancestors are very helpful and powerful. How powerful to find the queen, my soul mate from prison. I enjoy dancing with them daily. A soul with grace and dignity, this is how you should view yourself. How can it be against your religion to learn about the spiritual traditions of your ancestors? Africans have been misled to believe poverty is an individual failure rather than a carefully engineered system.

He who has the power to turn all negative vibes in his path into positive energy has learned the meaning of life. Not only do we honor our ancestors, but we live honorably because we are the future generations' ancestors.

Eye Am My Ancestors

Being conscious is the new gangster. Time to decolonize. Even the king needs teaching. You have nothing to worry about, just come to us in meditation. Our ancestors feel some type of way about you knowing the truth and still accepting religion. If you think spirituality is evil, you have been successfully indoctrinated by religion. If not, throw away the false teachings. You can't touch what you can't see. With my ancestors behind me, I am invincible.

Belief System

Family, our minds are the strongest. We have accepted false teachings to be dumbed down and drained. We been taught self-hatred, that we are ugly and all types of foolishness. That you are not worthy of direct contact with the high power, you must go through someone, a middleman.

All that power and belief you put in the God outside yourself, put it in your God Self. When I realized I was God, I was praying and talking to myself. Believe in your God Self. The greatest gift I received; I gave myself the day that I started believing in me unconditionally. In unity, multiple minds believing on one accord equals success. Activate.

I Am

I am not the body

I am not the emotion

I am not the thought

I am not the mind

The mind is merely an instrument of the soul

I am the soul

I am a spiritual being of divine intelligence Divine Love, Divine Power

I am one with my higher soul

I am that I am

Queen Dione

Another round of applause to my ancestors who found my soulmate. These things are actually easily done with Black power.

Letter to my Queen

My Queen, You Are Beautiful,

Wonderful Heavenly Sent

A Blessing You Are

Truly A Star Happiness to Us

In Black Power We Trust

We Live with Love Kisses and Hugs

Family Forever Always Together

Never Surrender

One's dignity may be assaulted, vandalized, and cruelly mocked. But it can never be taken away unless you surrender. African love created the entire human race, so if you hate Africans, you hate yourself. The truth doesn't change just because you don't understand or don't want to hear.

Three Things You Can't Hide for Long

The sun, the moon, and the truth. The best way to fight oppression and alien culture is to embrace your own.

Know thyself. We come from a long line of strength, honor, beauty, and intellect. There is power in unity and weakness in division. If you flinch from me calling you a king, queen, God, or Goddess you have been successfully programmed. The spirits of my ancestors didn't manifest into my soul bones to watch me become a convenient place for someone's feet. Black Power is not to be used negatively. You will be punished according to your actions.

You Create

- You create your own path
- You create your own meaning
- You create yourself by realizing yourself

Healing

The healing traditions of your ancestors are written in your DNA. All you need to do is activate them in a deep, spiritual desire to use them for the good of your people.

Queens and Kings

Ladies, if your respect for a king is based on how much he has in his pocket, you are not fit to be his queen/wife. Be his pillar of peace; the majority are already against him.

Be the type of queen that not only turn heads but souls as well. It's time for the brothas to start protecting the integrity of the Black women and show what Kings and Queens live like and grow together struggle together hustle together build together

Love Africa

You are not African because you are born in Africa. You're an African because Africa is born in you. It's in your genes and DNA...your entire biological makeup. Whether you like it or not, that's the way it is. However, if you were to embrace this truth with open arms, you will indeed be blessed with wonderful things. Despite all that was done to destroy the spirituality of our ancestors, it is still alive in the spirit of love.

Mindset

I Am an ancient soul in a modern body with a futuristic mindset. Our ancestors knew the power of music. Music is sound, music is vibration, vibrations cause everything to exist. Music can heal, affect moods, and alter your frequencies. Feel the universe's vibe. Trust in your own spirit. You have to win in mind to win in life.

MAC

I am here to make a change

To master all conversations

To make a living

To stop the killing

To win mentally over physically

Wake Up

We are a species with amnesia. Some have forgotten our roots and origins. We are quite lost in many ways. We live in a society that invests high amounts of money and vast quantities of energy ensuring that we all stay lost. A society that invests in creating unconsciousness, which invests in keeping people asleep so that we are just passive consumers of products and will not ask any questions.

Transformation

When you step out your mind and move into your soul, you open the door for your spirit. You open the door to magic. Speak what you seek until you see what you've said. When you're anointed by the spirit of your ancestors, you have this unstoppable look.

Discrimination

We had no bombs, no junk food, no stress, no sickness, no poverty, no crime rate, no pollution, and they called us primitive and savage. Just to force our people into ignorance of the unnaturals, wickedness, and sickness.

God's Hands

Do something for someone without telling the world you did it. You have never really lived until you have done something for someone who can never repay you.

Grand Risings

Let the flames of our ancestors burn so bright within, that the flames purify your soul while incinerating all the negative vibrations around you. Feel the energy within while meditating, and once you climax, hold on to that feeling forever.

Ancestor's Prayer

Our Great Afrikan parents who are amongst us, we humbly offer thanks for the Many blessings you have given. We extend our love to its ultimate state of being for the suffering that you have endured so that we may not suffer so Mothers of Afrikan Great Nation Fathers of our Afrikan selves.

We invoke you to further lead and guide us to a higher understanding of our true greatness and a more encompassing dedication of love for our Afrikan people. Parents of all Afrikan Children Guide us toward a greater unity Guide us in a stronger Afrikan Value system and lead us into the zenith of respect and love for our people, through Education and the Family Communal System

We swear upon the heritage and legacy that you have left us to uphold and sustain our rightful status on this Earth, and to continue the struggle for the mental and physical liberation of all Afrikan People

Asé

www.ingramcontent.com/pod-product-compliance
Lightning Source LLC
Chambersburg PA
CBHW052116110526
44592CB00013B/1639